Start to Finish
Second Series

FROM Seed TO Strawberry

● MARI SCHUH

LERNER PUBLICATIONS Minneapolis

Lerner Publications Company
A division of Lerner Publishing Group, Inc.
241 First Avenue North
Minneapolis, MN 55401 USA

For reading levels and more information, look up this title at www.lernerbooks.com.

Library of Congress Cataloging-in-Publication Data

Names: Schuh, Mari C., 1975–
Title: From seed to strawberry / by Mari Schuh.
Description: Minneapolis : Lerner Publications, 2015. | Series: Start to Finish, Second Series | Includes index. | Audience: Ages 5 to 8. | Audience: Grades K to 3.
Identifiers: LCCN 2015035566| ISBN 9781512409130 (lb : alk. paper) | ISBN 9781512413007 (pb : alk. paper) | ISBN 9781512410846 (eb pdf)
Subjects: LCSH: Strawberries—Life cycles—Juvenile literature.
Classification: LCC SB385 .S33 2015 | DDC 634/.75—dc23

LC record available at http://lccn.loc.gov/2015035566

Manufactured in the United States of America
1 – CG – 7/15/16

TABLE OF Contents

Strawberries are yummy! How do they grow?

First, gardeners find a space.

Strawberries do not need a lot of space to grow.
Gardeners can plant them in small gardens or
flower pots. Strawberries grow best in soil that
isn't too wet. They also need lots of sunlight.

Then gardeners plant seedlings.

Strawberries can grow from seeds. But gardeners usually use young strawberry plants called seedlings. They plant these seedlings with the **crowns** at the soil's surface. Then they water the seedlings.

Next, the seedlings become big plants.

The plants' short **roots** grow stronger. Gardeners water the plants. They get rid of weeds. They also **fertilize** the soil.

Stems called runners also grow.

The strawberry plants also **produce** runners. Runners grow along the surface of the soil. They grow small plants. The small plants can become new strawberry plants.

Tiny flower buds grow into white flowers.

Flower buds grow on the strawberry plants. The buds are small and light green. They grow in **clusters**. Soon they will turn into white flowers.

Then gardeners pinch off flowers.

Gardeners sometimes pinch off flowers for the first few weeks or for the entire first growing season. This allows the strawberry plants to get bigger and stronger. Later, the plants can grow more fruit.

Small strawberries grow.

More white flowers grow and open. Bees **pollinate** the open flowers. This helps the flowers produce strawberries. At first, the strawberries are small and green. Then they grow bigger.

Soon the strawberries can be picked.

The strawberries turn bright red. They are ready to be picked. People pick the strawberries along with their **caps** and stems. They pick them carefully so the berries will last longer.

Finally, the strawberries are ready to eat!

Strawberries can be eaten in many ways. Many people eat them fresh. They also use strawberries to make jam, jelly, and desserts. These sweet fruits are tasty and good for you!

Glossary

buds: flowers that have not yet opened

caps: several small green leaves that are attached to the top of a strawberry

clusters: groups of items that are close together

crowns: thick stems from which leaves, flowers, fruit, and runners grow

fertilize: to add something to soil to make plants and crops grow better

pollinate: to move pollen from one flower to another

produce: to create or bring forth

roots: the parts of plants that grow underground

runners: long, thin stems on strawberry plants that grow new plants

seedlings: small, young plants

Further Information

Colby, Jennifer. *Growing New Plants*. Ann Arbor, MI: Cherry Lake, 2014. Find out what plants need to grow and how they make new plants.

Lanz, Helen. *Strawberries*. Mankato, MN: Sea-to-Sea, 2012. Discover what you need to produce your own healthy strawberry plants.

Owings, Lisa. *From Strawberry to Jam*. Minneapolis: Lerner Publications, 2015. Follow each step in the process as strawberries become tasty jam.

Strawberry Facts for Kids
http://www.sciencekids.co.nz/sciencefacts/food/strawberries.html
This website has lots of fun facts about strawberries.

Strawberryville
http://www.strawberryville.com
Learn about strawberry nutrition, play games, and find strawberry recipes.

Index

Photo Acknowledgments
The images in this book are used with the permission of: © Angorius/Shutterstock.com, p. 1; © Tim UR/ Shutterstock.com, p. 3; © Carol Yepes/Getty Images, p. 5; © iStockphoto.com/YuriyS, p. 7; © EduardSV/ Shutterstock.com, p. 9; © Dorling Kindersley/Getty Images, p. 11; © iStockphoto.com/DLeonis, p. 13; © Brian Kinney/Shutterstock.com, p. 15; © PhotoAlto/Alamy, p. 17; © Clover No. 7 Photography/Getty Images, p. 19; © iStockphoto.com/Georgijevic, p. 21.

Front cover: Tim UR/Shutterstock.com.

Main body text set in Arta Std Book 20/26.
Typeface provided by International Typeface Corp.